When CREDIT MONEY *(far) Eclipses the* MONEY SUPPLY

A money-supply view of 21st Century Economic Disasters

TYMOTHY MARIS

Order this book online at www.trafford.com
or email orders@trafford.com

Most Trafford titles are also available at major online book retailers.

Printed in the United States of America.

ISBN: 978-1-4669-3398-9 (sc)
ISBN: 978-1-4669-3397-2 (e)

Trafford rev. 05/04/2012

 www.trafford.com

North America & international
toll-free: 1 888 232 4444 (USA & Canada)
phone: 250 383 6864 ♦ fax: 812 355 4082

AUTHORS' other books

IF A HOME HELD MEMORIES
Chapter 2: growing up years
—a snapshot autobiography via POETRY—

PREFACE

ACKNOWLEDGEMENTS

Special Thanks to:

My Brother Paul
Mom
Capital District Center

ACTUAL MONEY SUPPLY source:

www.federalreserve.gov

HOUSEHOLD INCOME source:

Dept. of Labor

Other sources:

Internet misc.

CONTENTS

CHAPTER 1

THE 1970'S

60'S COMMODITY STANDARD ABANDONMENT

With the coming of the 60's and 70's the Great National Net-Worth that was amassed post WWII during the late 40's and 50's, was eventually used up. We became a debtor Nation by the early 1980's.

- **From January 1960 to January 1970 the Actual Money Supply doubled (300 Billion Dollars to 600 Billion Dollars). That is a doubling in 10 years. Cash is most of this. See APPENDIX A.**

Money Supply was starting to be printed faster than population growth (note: the Actual Money Supply (cash, M1, M2, M3 etc) (APPENDIX A) used to keep pace with population growth). This creates Inflation.

With inflation rising, the Nation went off the Gold and Silver (commodity) standard (ie—1964 was the last year of 90% silver coins (ie—cash)). Paul Volcker was the architect of this abandonment.

RISE AND FALL—A NATURAL CYCLE (TO A POINT)

During President Nixons' administration in the early 1970's inflation was very high. The Dollar was devalued in 1971 and 1973 (Volcker again was the architect of this). When Ford took over as President in 1975 he tried to handle inflation by slowing the economy down. This created a severe recession in 1974-1975. Inflation was tamed but unemployment rose to almost 9 percent.

- **From January 1970 to January 1980 the Actual Money Supply almost tripled (590 Billion to 1.48 Trillion). It is notable that Cash expanded from 1960 to 1970 at a rate of 50 Percent in 10 years. And from 1970 to 1980 cash expanded almost double (100 Percent).**

The Stock Market meanwhile cycled from DOW 700 to 1000 several times. (See APPENDIX B). When Carter took over as President inflation was again rampant. In 1979 President Carter appointed Volcker as the head of the Federal Reserve. At this time interest rates were approaching or surpassing 14 percent per year. Volcker slowed the Actual Money Supply growth and allowed interest rates to rise. This tamed inflation but brought on the most severe recession (1982) since the Great Depression.

With inflation rising and falling and rising again, money was being printed to finance the current living standard (which tried to keep up to and surpass the Great 50's living standard). All the while money was leaving the United States (this would account for the Stock Market not rising with the Actual Money Supply growth as one might expect). This left the remaining money to slosh around in the Stock and Bond Markets. This went on until we hit what seemed to be a final Recession around 1982 (see APPENDIX B—the Stock Market sunk to the bottom again (DOW 800)). Doom and gloom (national bankruptcy) was rampant until President Reagan loosened the reign on the financial and banking markets (a credit money printing policy).

We were in the middle of the Vietnam war (60's to '76) and spending money that we did not have. Furthermore we were becoming more dependent on foreign OIL. The Oil embargo of the mid-70's just worsened things.

The same thing is happening today: Iraq and Afganistan war. MORE dependence on foreign OIL.

CHAPTER 2

THE 1980'S

**GIVEN: (credit) money was more or less non-existent at this point (1980's).
We were using Savings and
Actual Money Supply.**

LOOMING BANKRUPTCY

With bankruptcy looming a fearful Nation sent GOLD up to historic highs ($800 plus per ounce—January 1980). SEE APPENDIX D. (silver APPENDIX E, although there was a cornering of the silver market by the Hunt Brothers sending silver up past $40 per ounce briefly).

BEYOND BANKRUPTCY

- **From January 1980 to January 1985 the Actual Money Supply rose about 50 percent (1.48 Trillion Dollars to approximately 2.3 Trillion Dollars). See APPENDIX A.**

Federal Reserve Chairman Volcker had kept inflation under some control until he left in mid-1987.

REAGANOMICS

REAGANOMICS* for whatever reason (be it for lowering the expense of the National Debt, to increase the money flow, or to give the country another chance to get on its feet and WORK its IOUs away) started a (credit) money printing campaign. It solved the current problems of inflation and recession.

Greenspan took over the Chairman position in mid-1987, just before the 1987 Stock Market crash. Greenspan furthered the control of the Actual Money Supply. He is a great advocate of deregulation and balanced budgets.

- **From January 1985 to January 1987 the Actual Money Supply rose another 20 percent (2.3 Trillion to 2.75 Trillion). So far—much the same: a 10 percent increase every year.**

So we see with the 1987 crash (credit) money had NOT entered the system, due to the banking/financial deregulation.

The growth of the Actual Money Supply was directly reflected in the Stock Market price increase (DOW 800 in 1982 to DOW 2700 in 1987). It was also reflected in house price increases (for example the Author bought his first house in the 80's and 4 years later sold it for at least triple the buy price). But as stated earlier the Actual Money Supply grew about 20 percent (from 1980 to 1987).

The Stock Market quickly rose in 1987 to come in line with the Actual Money Supply.

** After the Federal Government lowered regulations per the savings and loan industry in the early 1980s, many financial entities expanded recklessly throughout the decade and later collapsed, requiring BAILOUTS by the Federal Government that cost the taxpayers around $500 billion.

MONEY PRINTING AND THE 1987 CRASH

The 1987 crash was the beginning of a larger Actual Money Supply printing cycle. This comeback and resumption of the upward spiral took a very few years. The Stock Market went from (DOW 800 to DOW 2700 in 1987, then DOW 2000, then by 1990 it was back to 2500) (see APPENDIX B), a 3.5 times (350 percent) increase. This is deemed quite plausible due to the Actual Money Supply of 3.17 Trillion.

- **From January 1987 to January 1990 the Actual Money Supply rose about 25 percent (2.75 Trillion to 3.17 Trillion).**
- **Between January 1980 to January 1990 the Actual Money Supply again doubles.**
- **This doubling continues unabated every decade.**

The Stock Market should have been at 3170 due to the Actual Money Supply, yet it was still at 2500, another recession (1990). The Actual Money Supply had yet to fully pull up the Stock Market. It eventually does pull up the Stock Market but the reigns on (credit) money seemed to loosen.

WORLD WIDE (CREDIT) MONEY PRINTING

Its given that the US Dollar was (and is) the World Wide Standard, for many items are based on it and many countries hold large sums of it.

When the US started printing (credit) money and greatly debasing the value of the Dollar many countries saw their holdings diminish in value (as was the case prior mentioned in post WWI Germany). One way to counter this was to print their own (credit) money (Countries who use the Dollar as their currency or pegged-their-currency-to-the-Dollar had to ride along with US led Inflation). This created a base for World Wide Inflation (based on the credit side) (and then as you can see by the 21st Century Economic Disaster, what goes up must come down). Another way to counter this diminishing value was to switch more and more of their holdings to other currencies.

POST WWI GERMANY (ALL OVER AGAIN)

The past seems to repeat itself. In order to get a glimpse of what the proposed REAGANOMICS policy does one can look at Post WWI Germany. During that period Germany had just signed over a massive debt obligation to the allies. Germany's economy was not doing well and for whatever reason they started a money printing campaign. Hyperinflation ensued in Germany and that massive debt, well let us just say it became less expensive.

CHAPTER 3

THE 1990'S

**GIVEN: (credit) money started to appear by January 1995.
By January 2000
(credit) money is estimated to be 6.3 Trillion.**

RECESSIONS AND (CREDIT) MONEY PRINTING

The 1990's saw their own share of recessions.

The massive (credit) money printing started. As prior noted in ABOUT THE AUTHOR, the Author, by the time 1997 and 1998 rolled around, estimated that the great (credit) money expansion would hit a peak in 6 to 8 years with a collapse to follow.

- **From January 1990 to January 1995 the Actual Money Supply grew About 10 percent (3.2 Trillion to 3.5 Trillion).**

- **From January 1995 to January 2000 the Actual Money Supply grew by approximately 33 percent (3.5 Trillion to 4.7 Trillion).**

- **Therefore from January 1990 to January 2000 the Actual Money Supply thus grew 43 percent.**

- **(credit) Money was starting to creep in.**

Meanwhile the Stock Market went from 2500 in January 1990 to 4000 in January 1995 (almost a double), and then from 4000 in January 1995 to 11000 in January 2000 (almost a triple). This amounts to the Stock Market going up 4.25 times (425 percent) from January 1990 to January 2000.

Seeing the Actual Money Supply grew at about 1.5 times (43 percent) we can see that the (credit) money (as reflected in the Stock Market) went up about 400 percent The National Debt probably grew a few Trillion (say 2 Trillion) at this time.[***]

[***] At this time I will note that (credit) money from outside the US enters the US via trade and the National Debt exacerbates the problem. This can be seen by the Asian collapse affecting this country.

The Actual Money Supply of $4.7 Trillion in the year 2000 gives rise to a Stock Market of DOW 4700 plus (credit) money of $6.3 Trillion equates to the DOW being at 11000.

Chairman Greenspan began a series of interest rate hikes in mid-1990 crying: unsustainable rates of growth in the US economy and overextended stocks, especially technology stocks.

- **The interest rate hikes must have accounted for the Actual Money Supply to NOT double this decade. This probably was an attempt to reign in the Credit Money expansion.**

By the summer of 1998 fear was building in regards to Asia and their (credit) money printing. The Great Asian collapse (felt worldwide, with many major markets taking a hit) occurred. The IMF (International Monetary Fund) helped out the Asian Countries. At the time the US government said that the Asian collapse would not be felt in the US, but it was felt as historians would tell you. Nonetheless it was a short blip down.

As stated prior the World Wide (credit) money printing was occurring, did occur, and in regards to Asia bubbled into a collapse. This collapse did not stop the (credit) money printing of the major economies (US, Europe etc) which we see fatefully bubbled into a collapse of their own (the 21st Century Economic Disaster).

CHAPTER 4

2000 TO 2008

GIVEN: (credit) money started to ramp up by January 2000:
it is estimated to be 6.3 Trillion Dollars.
The 2001-2003 crash erased much of this excess although some (credit) money
hide elsewhere. The latter 2000's saw a re-increase in (credit) money to bring it back
to a total of 6.6 Trillion Dollars.

RECESSIONS AND BLOWOFF (CREDIT) MONEY PRINTING

- From January 2000 to June 2003 the Actual Money Supply grew by approximately another 35 percent ($4.7 Trillion to $6 Trillion).

- The Actual Money Supply grew $1.8 Trillion to get us out of the 2001-2003 crash. It was needed to replace the (credit) Money destruction. We would otherwise have had a large economic deflation (of about 25 percent).

- From January 2000 to Sept 2008 the Actual Money Supply grew 120 percent (3.5 Trillion to 7.8 Trillion Dollars).

- But remember that the TOTAL (credit) money (from January 1995 onward to January 2008) seems to be 6.6 Trillion (DOW 7400 to 14000). We just set ourselves for another economic deflation (of about 40 percent this time).

- It is notable that holding back the Actual Money Supply last decade (1990's) did little to the (credit) Money. The (again)

doubling of the Actual Money Supply also did little to the (credit) Money.

... We were/are dependent on foreign OIL. We were/are dependent on foreign money. When OIL came down from $145 to $80 we saw a savings of $900 Billion per year. The money going out just comes back in via Foreign Investments (Stock and Bonds etc). We had/have a massive trade imbalance.

The price of GOLD went from $300 an ounce in 2000 to about $1020 in early 2008 (TRIPLE—note: OIL also tripled in this same time period). GOLD went from $450 in 2006 to about $1020 in early 2008 (that's about a 220 percent increase) to about $820 late 2008 (that's about a 190 percent increase) (See APPENDIX D). Noting that GOLD is a fear barometer of the money supply we nonetheless see that the trend-line is way up, just like the Stock Market. If GOLD just followed the Actual Money Supply growth it would be at approximately $660 per ounce (120 percent to Sept 2008).

The price of SILVER (which is a poor-mans barometer) more than tripled from 2000 to 2008 ($6 to $21) and then went way down (to $8.8 late 2008) (See APPENDIX E). If SILVER just followed the Actual Money Supply growth it would be at $13.2 per ounce (120 percent to Sept 2008).

Meanwhile the Stock Market went from 11000 in January 2000 to 8000 in January 2003 (a major drop—but it should have gone to DOW 6000. The remainder (2000) comprises (credit) money), and then from 8000 in January 2003 to 10000 in January 2004 (almost a 25 percent increase). It took another two years to get to 11000 again (about a 10 percent increase). That's only 3 short years to retrace the spiral back to DOW 11000. DOW 6700 is the floor for January 2006. All the rest is (credit) money.

The (credit) money and the Actual Money Supply expanded to get the US out of a major recession (2001-2003) that had not been seen since 1980.

Then the Stock Market went from 10000 in January 2004 to around 14000 in the early part of 2008. That's a MAJOR 40 percent increase in a short three and a half years. Or, if we look at it from January 2006, it went from 11000 to 14000. A MAJOR 30 percent increase, 3000 DOW points in the last year and a half of the three years. In the same time the Actual Money Supply grew

25 percent (6 Trillion in January 2004 to 7.4 Trillion in January 2008; that's 1.4 Trillion dollars; enough to seemingly cover 1400 DOW points (not the 4000). ****

The (credit) money keeps adding up. At sometime it is bound to crash due to this (credit) money creation from January 1995.

**** note—DOW retracement to 10000 in January 2004 saw an increase of the Actual Money Supply from 4.6 Trillion to 6.4 Trillion to cover the (credit) money destruction of 2001-2003 (DOW 11000 to DOW 8000). (just like we are trying to cover the (credit) money destruction now (DOW 14000 to DOW 8800)).

Now for the explanation:

1) 100% to 110% loans to house values

    If the 1980's and the 1990's weren't bad enough (yes the Author bought his second home at 90% loan to value), the 2000's turned absurd: buying with no money down, zero vested interest. Banks and homeowners were still banking on the great (credit) money printing. There was PMI (private mortgage insurance—on mortgages greater than 80%) but that didn't help.

2) stretching of future homeowner monthly debt payments (from 35% to 55% of monthly income)

    The 2000's saw more than its share of shaky homeowners getting into homes which were over their heads. Once again the Banks were responsible.

3) house values and home equity loans overreaching
    Sloppy assessments: again it was the Banks trying to bank on the great (credit) money printing.

4) teaser low rate variable mortgages

    Shaky homeowners with these mortgages just waiting for the teaser to disappear, leaving him over his head with payments. What were the Banks thinking?

5) Commercial Real Estate expansion: as of Nov 25 2008 no one is talking about other bubble in this arena.

6) Derivative Expansion: a stock market way of hiding the risk

A SECOND 21ST CENTURY DISASTER (THE 2007 2008 CRASH)

Waves of homeowners getting into trouble (ref: above 1 thru 4) probably was the straw that broke the camels back. (credit) money printing finally reached its zenith. There was no turning back, even with Fed interest rate reductions (too little too late. But it would have only delayed the inevitable collapse. (Where is the money coming from to propel the Stock Market (2000 in 1987 to 14000 in January 2008—see APPENDIX B) and the Real Estate Market up? (Credit Money) and partly Actual Money—as explained before its just plain money printing).

Home values started to sag turning the trickle into a stream. (1 thru 4) exacerbated the problem. The stock market started to sag from its peak of DOW 14,000.

The home debacle stream turned into a flood.

(credit) money printing in other aspects of the economy hit a wall. The reversal took Wall Street and the economy by storm.

The snowball kept growing until much of the (credit) money printing became suspect and tainted leading to bank failures.

Bank failures led to Main Street failures. Everybody was trying to mark-to-market questionable loans and good loans.

The Stock Market kept sinking (badly—as Oct swept in) making much of the (credit) money suspect. Now the good was being thrown out with the bad. Bailouts and buyouts couldn't stem the tide. The credit system went into cardiac arrest and even the good aspects of credit couldn't be had. States were in trouble, counties, cities and businesses such as GM.

The US troubles spread worldwide (badly—as Oct swept in).

The banks hoarded cash (did they have enough cash to meet a run-on-the-bank?).

As of (Oct 10 2008) the G7 will meet to (throw in the kitchen sink) to keep world stock markets from a meltdown.

As of (Oct 12 2008) the DOW rose 936 points because the G7 Governments threw billions into the banking system (the US threw 125 billion into the 9 largest banks and the remaining 125 billion into other financial entities (ie—buying preferred shares in the banks)) (thus the initial 250 billion, of the 700 billion (of the 1 trillion to date) is used up). To date it remains to be seen if the banks will not hoard this cash infusion.

As of (Oct 15 2008) the DOW dropped 733 points (see APPENDIX B).

If we mark-to-market now we will lose an estimated 600 billion (according to news sources) more (erasing much of the 700 billion bailout). The Banks do NOT want to mark-to-market in a sinking market for it will show a hit to their balance sheets.

Foreign governments are pouring 10's of Billions of dollars into their major banks (according to news sources). (credit) money has enveloped the whole world. As stated before, all major countries have been allowing the (credit) money to expand. These governments seem to be trying to replace this (credit) money with Actual Money Supply before the problem snowballs.

As of (Oct 21 2008) the Federal Reserve will open up $500 Billion of loans to the banking system.

As of (Oct 29 2008) the Federal Reserve lowered interest rates to approximately 1% thus increasing the Money Supply. This increases the Actual Money Supply.

As of (Nov 24 2008) the Federal Reserve Bails out Citi-Group. This is one of the largest US Banks. This Bailout is definitely needed to keep a large Financial domino effect from occurring. This effect entails large current job losses, large negative financial ripples and more turmoil in the Financial Market.

The US government seems to be trying to replace much of the bad (credit) money with actual money, either by printing or posting bonds and pulling in money from outside the US. This is needed to keep the US Real Estate and World Financial markets from collapsing and creating a much larger problem.

One can not say that the Commercial Real Estate Market is well. Only time will tell if this is another bubble waiting to burst. If it does watch out for many Mall closures.

CHAPTER 5

2008

A SETTLING PREDICTION

ONE—THE MONEY SUPPLY

The Actual Money Supply will grow from approximately 7.8 Trillion Dollars in Sept 2008. As noted before there seems to be 6.6 Trillion Dollars of (credit) money in the US system which needs to be replaced (or lost).^^

^^   Much of the hit will occur in the Stock and Real Estate Markets. Those who have margin accounts or mortgages from 1995 onward will take a hit on their down-payment positions (ie—lost actual equity besides lost profit equity). And those who bought with no-money-down will walk away and leave the negative positions for the banks and government to pick up with newly printed Actual Money Supply. Of course this means devaluation of the Dollar and everyone actually pays. With Real Estate Markets continuing to sag more people will lose their total equity (and then some) and will walk away from the house just as the no-money-down people did. It snowballs, so people must be helped to stay in their homes.

The lowering of interest rates to about 1 percent is like printing money and increases the Actual Money Supply.

Cash will be printed to increase the Actual Money Supply.

The Great BAILOUT will initially print some more money for the US (although posting a bond in and of itself is not money printing it brings money into the US from potential outside sources (ie—other countries which have printed more (credit) money.*)).

For example: lets say there is a country called AMERI and its currency is AMERI-DOLLARs. Through sloppy real-estate assessments and/or 110% loan-to-value loans the AMERI-DOLLAR money base (the actual money supply) grew at 1% this month. This actual money supply is deposited, at first in savings accounts. No one knew that the AMERI-DOLLAR had debased by 1% yet (ie—more AMERI-DOLLARs chasing the same amount of goods had yet to create inflation, thus debasing the money base. It also compounds upon itself.). Now let us say the savings account was used to buy US bonds. It is now an international problem (One example that comes to mind is the 1998 Asian collapse and how it brought down World Markets[**]).

[**] Note 1—the 1929 Stock Market collapse was caused by massive (credit) money printing in the US Stock Market

Note 2—the 1987 Stock Market crash was caused by a surge in the US Financial arena (most notably real estate)

Note 3—the 1998 Stock Market crash was caused by (credit) money printing and by Asian (credit) money printing

Note 4—the 2003 Stock Market crash was caused by (credit) money printing and the 9/11/2001 shock

Note 5—the 2008 Stock Market collapse was caused by the same (credit) money printing in Note 4 (it finally reached a peak)

TWO—THE STOCK MARKET

$1 TRILLION Dollar Bailout (does it support and equate to 1000 DOW points?). If we reference APPENDIX C, it does. As of Nov 24 2008 the actual Bailout is approaching $2 Trillion Dollars. This is being financed by (mostly) Bonds.

As of this writing:

1- (Oct 8, 2008—DOW below 10,000—see APPENDIX B for the OCT Chart)

2- (As of Oct 10, 2008—DOW around 8440, we lost 2.4 TRILLION Dollars (2400 points 22.1%-10,840 to 8,440)

3- (As of Oct 10, 2008—DOW around 8440, we lost 8.4 TRILLION Dollars in the past year (14,164 to 8,440)

4- (As of Nov 28, 2008—DOW around 8800

Past money printing (not credit money printing) and current National Debt will keep the Stock Market above DOW 6,000 (ie—blow-off to the downside) (Actual Money Supply seems to peg it at DOW 7800) with it settling in the (DOW 7,000 to 8,000 plus) range.).

The Author predicts current and future money printing will put the DOW around 9000 to 10000 plus.

DOW 10000 plus, is still absurdly high seeing the 70's and early 80's range was around 1000, but its predictable seeing the Actual Money Supply (cash, M1, M2, M3 etc) is growing (See APPENDIX A (Note:: the Actual Money Supply should have pegged the DOW to 1400 in 1980 instead of that horrible DOW 800).

THREE—THE REAL ESTATE MARKET

As of the end of Sept 2008 the median price of a home is $189,000.

Sept 2008 Real Estate fell an average of 17 percent of the home value. That's 17 percent in ONE month.

One estimate shows, as of Oct 2008, the total inventory of houses for sale is equal to a ONE YEAR supply.

So-called Mega Mansions (median house value of $300,000 plus) are not selling well, just like high-end consumer products.

If homeowner (includes speculation houses) Real Estate bubbled up as far as the Stock Market we should fall on average 40 percent. Overbuilding and speculation may push prices down further in the frothy market areas. This pulls down Real Estate values in general and will feed upon itself until it levels out.

Commercial Real Estate may soon fall victim to a devastating crash when stores can not make ends meet and then close. This is a result of shoppers not buying. (note: Macys and Coach stock prices are down at least 50 percent, while Wal-Mart is holding up).

Consumers will be pulling in the reigns all around seeing they are facing a lower standard of living. This will be reflected in Real Estate prices.

FOUR—TAXES (AND REBATES)

There will initially be a REBATE (on income taxes) to stimulate the economy. This will be paid for by Bonds or just increasing the money supply or maybe an income tax increase elsewhere.

Taxes will be going up for many people. There is talk of $250,000 income per year as being the break-off point for tax increases.

WHAT'S TO COME

Americans will have to face a lower standard of living in the near term. Taxes WILL go up (either the income tax will increase or the inflation-tax will increase* (note: inflation IS a tax on EVERYONE who has dollars).

* The increased deficit and Money Supply Growth will erode the Dollar. This will make the Dollar fall, at first glance. Other countries will be increasing their money supply too, sometimes faster than the U.S. Money Supply. This 'sometimes faster' will make the Dollar seem to rise. But it is all relative. All if not most currencies will be eroding thus giving rise to world wide inflation.

The National debt is at a staggering $30,000 per every man, woman and child in the United States (approximately 10.8 Trillion Dollars) (as of 10/22/08 Presidential hopefuls economic plans will add 3 to 5 Trillion Dollars to the National Debt (according to news sources)).

The $1 Trillion Bailout package will cost approximately $3,000 more per every man, woman and child when enacted (ie—more US Bonds being issued). Hopefully the $3,000 will be paid back in the not-so-near-future. Hopefully some of the $3,000 will be paid back soon when the mark-to-market shows there was some value in some of the distressed loans.

- **The $1 Trillion BAILOUT will package will grow, to $2 Trillion, $3 Trillion etc. In one way or another this will be printed money (Actual Money Supply): Just like the $500 Billion to get out of the 1987 crash, just like the $1.8 Trillion to get out of the 2003 crash.**

In perspective: the 2003 crash lost $3 Trillion of Stock Market Value. This 21st Century Disaster lost about $8 Trillion of Stock Value (at the low of Dow 6000).)

- **Shall we estimate the BAILOUT to be $4+ Trillion this time.**

Unfunded National Obligations approach a massive $100 Trillion Dollars. These Obligations for the most part comprise Social Security and larger still Medicare. Unfortunately to help close the gap there will be large cutbacks. Furthermore actual Money printing will deflate the actual value of the $100 Trillion thus closing the gap.

The Actual American Net Worth will be permanently set back (ie—lower equity (stock, IRA, etc) value, lower home value, lower cash value (ie-inflation), possible higher Federal, State and local taxes, possible higher property taxes, and higher item prices (ie-inflation)).

The Actual American Safety Net (Social Security and Medicare) will be permanently set back.

Meanwhile, Americans should invest what little they have left wisely. If you didn't get out during the sweeping downturn its too late, so just hold on. If you did get out, or have more money to invest and you want to invest again in the Stock Market try investing in technology or the remaining financial institutions. Otherwise try investing in beaten up commodities (note: as of 10/22/08 spot gold and silver have high markups (ex—silver $9.77 per oz, 1 oz silver coin is $16+), even if you could find some on the spot market (Note: bulk Futures Market—1 contract (2,500 oz silver) is going to cost you at least $25,000) or even time tested artwork.

Do not believe that the DOW will again hit 14000 in the near future, unless of course the US Government unwisely resurrects the (credit) money printing machine or prints TRILLIONS of dollars. For the DOW at its current position has wrung out a lot of the excess (credit) money printing and then some (the then some has been replaced by US Bonds (the BAILOUT) to keep the housing market and the stock market up a bit so that much of the good would be saved).

MARCH 2012 ADDENDUM

American are now at a lower Standard of Living. Here we are 3+ YEARS later and unemployment is just now dropping from 9.5% to 8.5%. Wages are stagnant. Gasoline is back up. Prices of most things (excluding housing—read on) are up double digit (Inflation Tax—mentioned in CHAPTER 5).

The National DEBT has increased to $ 15+ TRILLION, up from $10.8 TRILLION. In February 2012 the U.S. Government almost defaulted on its debt seeing it couldn't (print) more Bonds to finance the continuing bailout.

- **The $1 TRILLION bailout has grown to $4+ TRILLION. Most of it is printed money. The Actual Money Supply has grown from $7.8 TRILLION to $12 TRILLION: the U.S. Government refuses to acknowledge it (ie: M3 reporting has ceased).**

The $4+ TRILLION in printed money has hurt everyone holding REAL DOLLAR ASSETS (Long Term Bonds etc—a 40% loss in real value)::

1- (ie: CHINA's $5 TRILLION in Bonds is now worth $3 TRILLION (better this than nothing left));

The $4+ TRILLION in printed money has neither helped nor hurt everyone holding PAPER DOLLAR ASSETS (40% loss in real value plus a 40% gain in Inflation value netting a zero gain)::

1- Commercial Real Estate prices (real prices are 40% less).

2- House prices (real prices are 40% less). They would have fallen 50% but only fell (on average 10%) due to printed money Inflation. Imagine House prices falling 50%—people would walk away in droves from their houses (most house prices would have been below mortgage prices). (ie: homeowners HAVE lost 50% due to the housing glut and the Inflation Tax (better this than nothing left));

3- The Stock Market has come back from 8000 to 13,000, less of course zero (0) income tax due to regained losses. But those banks who used the Bailout money to buy stock at 8000 have made money (furthermore the U.S. Government has said they did not have to pay income taxes on it—another gimme). This covers their inflation loss and keeps them solvent.

4- Even the National DEBT has inflation adjusted to a zero (0) increase.

The $4+ TRILLION in printed money has helped everyone holding HARD DOLLAR ASSETS (40% gain in Inflation value)::

1- Those holding GOLD and SILVER and other liquid commodities have retained most of their real dollar value (GOLD and SILVER have doubled (800 to 1600 and 16 to 34 respectively), less, of course—income tax when you sell it).

**The U.S. Government and other countries have dug out of this world-wide default
by massive-inflation-reallocation-of-money
(via printing money).**

The BIG 5 (most BONDS, all Money Supply, all Real Estate, all Stock Markets, all Entitlements) have taken a re-allocation hit. Credit Money couldn't slosh (hide) anywhere this time.

CREDIT MONEY IS (mostly) GONE!!!! Everyone who is going to pay for it has already done so. Prices will increase AGAIN LOCKSTEP with (printed) Actual Money Supply. Remember those low interest rates. They help keep the printing going.

SO WHO RECEIVED THE MONEY?? (A RE-CAP)

It was not long-term bondholders or long-term holders of cash. It was not stockholders who sold on the way down in October 2008. It was not SPEC house or regular house owners who sold greater-than-20% off 2008 prices.

It was GOLD, SILVER, OIL and other liquid commodities investors (they actually made money (excluding gasoline (See APPENDIX C) it is almost a break even now (gasoline 4.5 dollars per gallon))). It was stockholders who bought at the October 2008 low (ie—Banks) (they actually made money). It was those who received government GRANTS (they actually made money). It was those who did NOT sell their stock or house or other Real Estate, up to this point (they almost broke even***).

*** note again:: if there was no money printing**** they would have lost 40 to 50 percent instead of todays 10 percent. The money printing filled-the-gap between what people wanted for their Real Estate (etc) (todays 10 percent off) and what they actually would have received (40 to 50 percent off) if there was no money printing.

**** money (printing):: creating cash or M1, M2, or M3 (or what I would say—M4): all in all as I said in the 1990's 'MONEY MONEY' (vs. 'CREDIT MONEY').

WAGE-EARNERS DID NOT RECEIVE THE MONEY

Wage Earners (ref: APPENDIX H—"household" income (not per person income)) did NOT receive much of the windfall since 2008:: (the lowest 80% actually saw a drop in income (the 95th percentile saw a rise in income of only 810 dollars)). For example===== the 20th percentile mark went down ($20,712 in 2008 to $20,000 in 2010); the 40th percentile mark ($39,000 in 2008 to $38043); the 60th percentile mark ($62,725 in 2008 to $61735 in 2010); the 80th percentile mark ($100,240 in 2008 to $100,065); THE TOP FIVE PERCENT MADE SOME MONEY!!! The poor got poorer!!! The middle class is becoming POOR.

Prior to 1980, when the Actually Money Supply doubled every 10 years, all income brackets (percentile marks) doubled every 10 years. After 1980 incomes failed to keep up with the doubling money supply!!! Now let us take a CLOSER look at, say, the 60th percentile mark ========== 1970 to 1980: income went up 100%; 1980 to 1990 income went up 80%; 1990 to 2000 income went up 48%; 2000 to 2010 income went up 42%;

In effect most wage earners are NOT receiving a fair share of the current Actual Money Supply. There is no replacement from other sources (pensions are worth less, savings are worth less, stocks are worth less, houses are worth less, gasoline did not go down (and stay down), food and clothing etc did not go down, etc).

TABLES

YEAR	Money Supply (M1, M2, M3) from www.federalreserve.gov.	**A**
1960	> > (300 billion)	
1962		
1964		
1966		
1968		
1970	>>>> (600 billion)	
1972		
1974		
1976		
1978		
1980	>>>>>>>> (1.48 trillion)	
1982		
1985	>>>>>>>>>> (2.3 trillion)	
1987	>>>>>>>>>>>> (2.7 trillion)	
1988		
1990	>>>>>>>>>>>>>>> (3.17 trillion)	
1992		
1995	>>>>>>>>>>>>>>>>> (3.5 trillion)	
1996		
1998		
2000	>>>>>>>>>>>>>>>>>>>>>>> (4.7 trillion)	
2003	>>>>>>>>>>>>>>>>>>>>>>>>>>>> >>>> (6 trillion) (no more M3	
2004	Reporting)	
2006		
2008	>>>>>>>>>>>>>>>>>>>>>>>>>>>>>>>>>>> (7.8 trillion)	
2010		
2012	>>>>>>>>>>>>>>>>>>>>>>>>>>>>(est. 14 trillion)>>>>>>>>>>>>>	
2014		

YEAR	DOW (stock market—biggest 30 stocks)	**B**
1960	> > (700)	
1962		
1964		
1966		
1968		
1970	>>>> (1000)	
1972		
1974	>> (700)	
1976		
1978	>>>> (1000)	
1980	>> (800)	
1982		
1985	>>>>>>>> (1500)	
1987	>>>>>>>>>>>>> (2700)	
1988	>>>>>>>>>> (1739)	
1990	>>>>>>>>>>>> (2500)	
1992		
1995	>>>>>>>>>>>>>>>>>>>> (4000)	
1996		
1998		
2000	>> (11000)	
2003	>>>>>>>>>>>>>>>>>>>>>>>>>>>> >> (8000)	
2004	>>>>>>>>>>>>>>>>>>>>>>>>>>>>>>>>>>>> (10000)	
2006	>> (11000)	
2008	>>>(14000)>>>>>>>>>>> . . . . oct 8 2008 (10000)>>>>>>>>>>>>>>>>>>> . . . . oct 10 2008 (8440)>>>>>>>>>>>>>> . . . . nov 28 2008) (8800)>>>>>>>>>>> . . . . early 2009 (6547)>>>>> . . . . june 2009 (8500)>>>>>>>>>	
2010	>>>>>>>>>>>>>>>>>>>>>>>>>>>>>>>>>>>>>>(10000)	
2012	>>>>>>>>>>>>>>>>>>>>>>>>>>>>>>>>>>>>(13000)>>>>>>>>>	

YEAR	GASOLINE (nominal)	**C**
1960	> (.35 per gallon)	
1962		
1964		
1966		
1968		
1970	>	
1972		
1974	>> (.50 per gallon)	
1976		
1978	>>> (.75)	
1980	>>>> (1.00) (1981 peaks at 1.35)	
1982		
1985	>>>> (1.00)	
1987	>>>> (1.00)	
1988	>>>>	
1990	>>>>	
1992		
1995	>>>>	
1996	>>>>> (1.25)	
1998	>>>> (1.00)	
2000	>>>>>>> (1.50)	
2003	>>>>>> (1.40)	
2004	>>>>>>> (1.50)	
2006	>>>>>>>>>> (2.00)	
2008	>>>>>>>>>>>>>>>>>>> (3.25) (peaks over 5.00) early 2009 >>>>>> (2.25)	
2010	>>>>>>>>>>>>>>>>> (2.50)	
2012	>>>>early 2012>>>>>>>>> (3.25) . . . . mid 2012 >> (4.40)	

YEAR	GOLD	**D**
1960	>	
1962		
1964	>> (34)	
1966		
1968		
1970	>>>>	
1972		
1974		
1976		
1978		
1980	>>>>>>>>>>>>>>>>>>>>>>>> (800+)	
1982		
1985	>>>>>>>>>>>>> (400)	
1987	>>>>>>>>>>>>>	
1988		
1990	>>>>>>>>>>>>>>>	
1992		
1995	>>>>>>>>>>>>>>	
1996		
1998		
2000	>>>>>>>> >>>>> (300)	
2003		
2004		
2006	>>>>>>>>>>>>>>>>>>>>>>>>>>>>>>>>> (1020)	
2008	>>>>>>>>>>>>>>>>>>>>>>>>>>>> (820) . . . . oct 2008>>>>>>>>>>>>>>>(740) . . . . 2009>>>>>>>>>>>>>>>> (900)	
2010	>> (1200) . . . . 2011>>>>>>>>>>>>>>>>>>>>>>>>>>>>>>>>>>>>>>(1900)	
2012	>>> (1700)	
2014		

YEAR	SILVER	**E**
1960	>	
1962		
1964	>> (1)	
1966		
1968		
1970	>>>>	
1972		
1974		
1976		
1978		
1980	>>> (40+)	
1982		
1985	>>>>>> (4)	
1987	>>>>>>>	
1988		
1990	>>>>>>> (5)	
1992		
1995	>>>>>>>> (6)	
1996		
1998		
2000	>>>>>>>> (6)	
2003		
2004	>>>>>>>>>>	
2006		
2008	>>>>>>>>>>>>>>>>>>>>>> (21) . . . . oct 2008>>>(8.8) . . . . 2009>>>>>> (16)	
2010	>>>>>>>>>>>>>>>>>>>>>>>>>>>> (28) . . . . 2011>>>>>>>>>>>>>>>>>>>>>>>>>>>>>>>>>>>>>(50)	
2012	>>>>>>>>>>>>>>>>>>>>>>>>>>>>>>>>>> (34)	
2014		

| YEAR | House-hold Income source: Dept. of Labor | | | | | H |
	Households (in thousands)	percentile marks=== 20th	40th	60th	80th	the 95th
1960						
1962						
1964						
1966						
1968						
1970	64778	3688	7065	10276	14661	23175
1972						
1974						
1976						
1978						
1980	82368	7478	14024	21500	31480	50661
1982						
1985						
1987						
1988						
1990	94312	12500	23662	36200	55205	94748
1992						
1995						
1996						
1998						
2000	108209	17920	33000	52174	81766	145220
2003						
2004						
2006						
2008	117181	20712	39000	62725	100240	180000
2009	117538	20453	38550	61801	100000	180001
2010	118682	20000	38043	61735	100065	180810
2014						

Printed in the United States
By Bookmasters